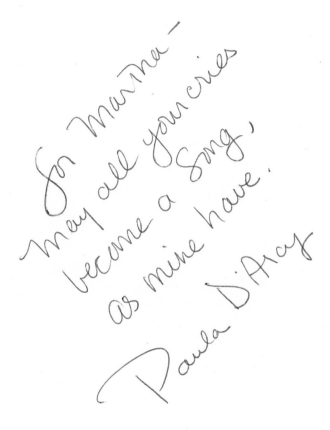

For Martha —
May all your cries
become a song,
as mine have.

Paula D'Arcy

SONG FOR SARAH

SONG FOR
Sarah

A Young Mother's
Journey Through Grief and Beyond

Paula D'Arcy

Harold Shaw Publishers
Wheaton, Illinois

Scripture quotations are from the Revised Standard Version of
the Bible, copyright 1946, 1952, 1971 by the Division of Christian Education of the National Council of the Churches of
Christ in the USA, and used by permission.

ISBN 0-87788-762-4

Cover design by David LaPlaca

Library of Congress Cataloging-in-Publication Data

D'Arcy, Paula, 1947-
    Song for Sarah : a young mother's journey through grief
and beyond / Paula D'Arcy.
      p.   cm.
    ISBN 0-87788-762-4
    1. Consolation. 2. D'Arcy, Paula, 1947-   . 3. Grief—
Religious aspects—Christianity. 4. Children—Death—
Religious aspects—Christianity. I. Title.
BV4907.D37 1995
248.8'6'092—dc20   95-10816
                                       CIP

---

02 01 00 99 98 97 96 95

10 9 8 7 6 5 4 3 2 1

for Megan, Max, Michael, Marguerite, Paul
for Peter
and especially for Sarah

I thank Meredith Powers,
for the use of the poem on page ix,
written for her infant son, Max;

Paul Fanelli, for his photography;

The Robert DeFosse Studio, Farmington,
Connecticut, for film processing;

Sheldon Vanauken,
for his personal encouragement and help;

Donald Kauffman,
The Foundation for Christian Living,
who first believed this Song should be published;

My friends, especially Billy, Ray, Marilyn, Carolyn,
Ann, Bev and Nell;

My family, and Roy's,
for their support which still continues.

"... I sang him a lullaby,
an unfinished lullaby,
a raspy, whispered lullaby
that made his blue eyes smile."

Meredith Powers

Sarah, July 1975

Foreword

Nothing can prepare us for the cruel loss, the unbearable pain, that comes when we lose a loved one.

Such grief breaks open the heart and lays bare the soul. Our lives are changed forever . . . we can never again be as we were before. All extraneous things are stripped away, and we are brought face to face with life's most bitter lesson.

In our despair, we struggle . . . just to "survive"! Our hearts have been broken, and the only way they can ever be healed is for us to reach out to help others who are also traveling along the same path of grief.

Paula D'Arcy has done this in writing *Song for Sarah*. She has taken her sorrow and transformed it into a gift of love that will bring peace and comfort to those who grieve.

When I first held *Song for Sarah* in my hands, I was at the lowest point of my life. My beloved son, Todd, had just died, suddenly and unexpectedly, and my safe, happy, familiar world had been totally destroyed! I saw no Hope ahead. . . . I had lost someone too precious to me! I didn't think I could go on living.

During the early days of my sorrow, other books on grieving had been given to me, but not one of them truly comforted me until my daughter, Joy (who had also lost her infant son, Gideon, the year before), gave me *Song for Sarah*. Reading this simple journal finally brought me a measure of the peace I so desperately needed.

As I read Paula D'Arcy's words, written directly from her own shattered heart (with complete honesty and simplicity), for the first time I was able to realize that someone else had walked this same terrible terrain of pain that *I* was now walking and that, somehow, she had found the strength to "survive" and had discovered a way back to Life.

I needed to *know* that I, too, could go on, and perhaps, one day, come back to Light . . . to Hope, after these long, dark hours of Despair.

Paula D'Arcy has given totally of herself in relating this agonizing experience. She has held nothing back. Her heart was torn open, and her sorrowing spirit was revealed to us in the writing of this journal . . . begun with such love and completed with such courage.

Reading her words, I realized that here, at last, in the midst of my anguish, was a "Light" by which I might see again, a voice that spoke the Truth, and an under-standing heart, whose deep sorrow matched my own. With her help . . . I took the first steps toward healing.

Joan Walsh Anglund

Introduction

These letters for my daughter, Sarah, are part of the actual journal I began in 1973 when I first learned that I was pregnant. I little guessed then that within two and a half years they would be my detailed recollection of a time and a life that was suddenly and unkindly ended. And yet the pain and outrage of death eventually brought me such insight and growth that these words for Sarah truly became not a cry, but a song.

Today, three years since the death of my husband and daughter, I live a full and warm life with my second child, Beth Starr, in the same town where Roy, Sarah, and I began our home, still surrounded by a close community of loving friends. And yet a real part of our lives will always be the fact that we are the survivors. Our living is, and will be, an unfinished song—a memory of the life which Roy and I had dreamed of so expectantly, and which we had so briefly begun to share.

So many wonderful people joined to make up the memory; together they were a beautiful part of our lives. But the initial dream which allowed these memories was

Roy's and mine. And so it should not truly be I alone, but Roy and I together, who offer this song: a remembrance of a love and a family which was, for a special moment in time, uniquely ours.

Dear Unborn Child:

Really, dear Andrew (I'm sure you're an Andrew. And I am really, truly *pregnant!* What was just an everyday diagnosis for a busy obstetrician is a word which changes my whole life). I don't know the words to express my heart's excitement. Such a joyful secret! Welcome, welcome, welcome—tiniest baby. Grow strong inside me.

MARCH, 1973

Dear Andrew:

It's still hard to believe that a "little you" is really there. Your father is probably not thinking about you as constantly as I am, but then you are happening in *this* body, not his. Still, I notice the way he tells people that we are "expecting." He's proud. He's glad of us, and even a bit incredulous that there will be "you." I don't know if it's right to say that he's awed by our news, but he has *some* special feeling (I see it on his face) as if to him your coming is almost a miracle.

Your father views us, and everything, as part of the whole process of life. His mind is endlessly searching life for answers. He wonders about the principles which have motivated man's often incomprehensible history. But while I admire his questions, it is not the same for me. What is real to me is *here,* not a thousand years ago on some northern plain. I am moved by this body, which gently changes to carry another human life. Think of that! I am almost not able to comprehend that within me a mind and a soul are alive, someone separate from myself.

Yet this, for me, is enough. There is no need to relate us to anyone or anyplace. I feel little need for the Bible your father reads from his rocking chair each day. The stories seem too remote. The essence of life is surely here. I am sustained by all our love.

Dear Andrew:

It's beginning to feel like spring. Your father has started a tray of pepper plants in our south dining room window. Will I really eat one some night this coming winter while holding onto you? Will you be real one day?

Your father and Joe and Pat (What "uncles" you'll have!) went to Maria's Luncheonette today for their usual chili. Your dad said they talked about you and the difference you'll make in our lives. We'll love it when you come. Together we want you.

I think that makes a difference. You are not your father's idea. Or mine. But ours. We wouldn't think of you without us all together. A family.

Dear Andrew:

Why can't I look enormous? If you're there (and the doctor promises that you are) then I want to look full of you. Everyone ought to know you're on your way. I don't appreciate looking just slightly fat. I want to look positively pregnant. Poke out, why don't you?

This night I've begun to sew the casing for your bassinette. Me, preparing a room for our baby! I love to walk in your room. I dream for you.

Dear Andrew:

It's kinda scary, like tempting fate, but I bought you some clothes today. If I refold them and hold up each item one more time for your father's approval, they'll be worn out before you arrive. Everything is blue, so I hope you're you! I've stacked your shirts in little piles, just so.

I've hung your mobile. I smooth the diapers. I hug the stuffed toys. Then I sit and look at my belly. I love carrying you.

Your father is working so hard on our first vegetable garden. He faithfully records the seeds he plants for future harvest, much as I record all my first introductions to you. But I lack your father's patience. I rush with almost everything. There is so much restlessness within me. On June 1 your father wrote in his garden record that "Patience is another harvested food from the garden; determination another crop. Bounty comes, if at all, in its own good time."

I am not in control of this newness about me. Nature, and the hours, will have their way.

Dear Andrew:

This morning I patched your father's jeans. Then just
you and I took such a long walk. We are so close. Your
father says I'm an incurable romantic. Is that why I'm
starting to cry about our shortly never being so close
again? From the second you're born, you'll begin to pull
away and start your own life. For just a little while
longer it's *us*.

Dear Andrew:

How can I feel two opposites at once? I don't want this
pregnancy ever to be over. I love living so near you. But
when will it end? I'm so tired. Haven't I been big-bellied
forever?

Our garden is full of crops that want my care. Two
hundred tomatoes tonight—and all those zucchini to cut
off the vines. And you're in my way, a nuisance to every
chore that needs me. Everything keeps growing so fast.
You too! You can be so heavy.

Dear Andrew:

The problem is, how am I going to know when "labor" is real? I will just fold up with embarrassment if I call the doctor and I'm wrong. Please, God, strike me with unmistakable signs so that I can be sure. If it's all too subtle I'm so afraid I'll miss my cue. Remember, Lord, I can be awfully thick.

And I can be awfully hungry. Please, God, am I hungry! I never want to see celery or lettuce again. They only make my hungrier. My dream is to find a vast bar of chocolate.

Dear Andrew:

This is really the pits. I'm knitting this little red blanket for you, but I can't concentrate. I have these cramps, sort of. I *think* maybe this is it. But is it?

But then just yesterday the doctor said it could be a while. Oh, brother. And yet, if it's *not* labor, then why do I have funny cramps? I'd give anything to be smart right now. My grandmother was right about me all along. No common sense.

[Two hours later.] Betsy answered my "Help!" and came over to observe me. Can't somebody help me decide? "I've had two kids myself," she says. "If it were happening to me, I'd know. But this is you. I can only say you *look* ready. But . . ." Pregnant women decide alone.

Well, I'd better call. If it's only abdominal flu then I'll have to live with it. Thank God there can only ever be *one* first time.

Dear Andrew:

You're Sarah! I can't believe it! First we're laughing, then
we're crying. We can't believe it. I *was* right about the labor, and not with a lot of time to spare! We laughed,
walking into the hospital. I felt so embarrassed, so obvi-
ous with my suitcase. We kept saying, "This is it!" We
laughed till it hurt—then we worked hard to breathe
you out. The end was so fast—you insistent; me scared.
And your daddy tripping to get into his delivery room
"whites." And then you. Ten fingers, ten toes, little you.
Perfect you.

Watching you stretch your way into this world was
the fullest joy I've ever known. Complete. No happiness
in my life has ever been that true. I'll carry your first cry
with me everywhere I go.

Now you suck softly at my breast. I sing you quiet
lullabies. How I love you.

Dear Sarah:

What's happening? Why are you crying? And why can't I figure out why you're crying? I thought I was as cool and capable as they came. But look at me. Who'd have guessed being a parent wasn't easy? I love you till I think I'll burst, but you still get me turned all upside down. What an adjustment from merely being someone's daughter to also being someone's (your!) mother. It's overwhelming that you depend so totally on me.

In the hospital motherhood all seemed adventurous and exciting. But here at home I'm way too tired to be poetic. Some days it's a contest to see who cries more, you or I. How lucky we are that your daddy is so uncomplaining.

Dear Sarah, do you think we'll make it?

Dear Sarah:

Was I the one who secretly doubted that one little baby could significantly change our lives? And so, I had a lot to learn! We are indeed *very* different with you! The days that were ours have all become yours. You first. "Sarah's schedule" has become the ruling almanac of our week—or at least of mine.

Your father's life is a lot less changed. He is still perpetually reading books and avoiding the stacks of papers which beg his correction—an English teacher who hates to grade! I'd mark the essays immediately just to get them out of my way, off my mind. But no piece of paper creates a pressure upon your daddy's nerves. It is only I, your mother, who feels buried by all that needs to be done. One carton in that cluttered place your father calls his "study" bears the label "Student Themes— 1972". There they wait to be mailed. I want to moan every time I trip over the box. But your father is wholly unconcerned. It wouldn't ever stop him from chatting with friends or watching a rerun of a good Humphrey Bogart film. That we might rent his serenity, little daughter! Let's hope you'll capture some for your own.

Dear Sarah:

Was I really as harried as those thoughts I just re-read from November? It seems so much better now. I mean, I'm far from a pro, but I do think I'm getting used to us. Did I often make it hard for you, those first months? There I was trying to soothe you with one arm, furiously turning the pages of my *Dr. Spock* with the other. I really apologize for being so new and shaky!

Please promise me that you'll grow up and realize that the problem was never my not loving you. My feelings would surely explode if I loved you any harder. I never dreamed what it could be to love my own child so deeply.

Dear Sarah:

Those early anxious days seem farther and farther removed now. You and your father and I have become such a team. Who could want more than our simple life, which is so full?

So much began inside of me from the moment you swelled my belly with love. You must have sown my first seed of patience, for I see how I am beginning to change. I look at my life and I want it to be good. I want to give away the overflow of love you and your daddy and I feel. Some days this house just rings with our love. And because of the way we feel about our home, we're planning to baptize you right here in our living room. We'll dedicate you to God right in the same rooms where we eat and laugh and visit with your friends.

It's hard, Sarah, to lead a Christian life. The world moves so fast beyond these simple walls. We're lucky to be sitting here, waiting for the bread dough to rise, and to have our big fight of the week be "who gets the last chocolate chip cookie." I hope you'll never take it lightly when we pray with you. Or when we hold you at the window to watch the birds and squirrels.

Your daddy wrote a poem about us which says that we three are like a strong tree with good roots. One of us alone would be buffeted by the wind. But together we're strong.

You two nourish me with your love.

Dear Sarah:

Today we spent two hours sitting on the redwood table blowing bubbles. Me. A year ago I would have felt too rushed by my chores and obligations to sit and play such a game. How you've helped to slow me down.

Now I tend all of us as carefully as those garden seeds we want to grow. I fuss less about incidental things and care more about how *people* are affected. I like to size things up by saying, "In the whole of my life, does this really matter?" That helps me to put many silly things aside.

Dear Sarah:

There you are, sleeping just beyond my door. I get the
red badge of courage today for taking you to your first
swimming class at the Y. You looked almost starved next
to the other babies in the class! I just don't realize how
tiny you are until I see you with others.

How did the water really feel? Do you have *any* idea
what it takes to submerge a six-month-old baby? Your
father shook his head at our story. He said he couldn't
even have watched. But you were a champ! Another of
life's beginnings.

While you sleep, your father is in the basement,
busy on a new woodworking project. Grow up with his
temperament, Sarah. How lovingly he sands the wood
pieces; how patiently he imagines how he can work
them together. I still sit and look at the jewelry box he
made for me when you were born—so intricate and perfect. Like you.

Do you sense this harmony of ours? Do you feel the
way we work together? Are you happy? How fortunate
we are, we three!

Dear Sarah:

My craving for chocolate while I was pregnant no doubt helped to create the "hot rod" you are becoming. Sometimes it takes both your father *and* me just to hold you flat in order to change a diaper. How you love to move! You're swimming so well now. I love going extra times to give you new chances to flip through that water. Why did I ever hesitate about taking you? Let's hope I never hold you back from anything you want to do. I only want to enable you to risk, to dare to try. Such a life you may know!

Will you dream? I dream a lot. I won't kid you. We do live from bill to bill here, always praying that nothing will break down. I asked your father tonight if he thought we'd look back on all our budgeting someday, and laugh and say, "Boy, those were the good days!" He said we might look back, but how could it ever seem funny?

We laughed. But I wonder. Something here is so good, even if we're just barely getting by. I guess it's that *we* are here. There's joy in that.

Dear Sarah:

Some weeks it's hard to steal even a few minutes to write. You fill my days. I have despaired of you ever cutting teeth. You are so late with them. But you *may* creep. At least you are as close to creeping as you can be without actually going. And then won't the fun begin!

I gave your daddy his birthday gift today, a baby backpack carrier. I can see you two already, off to explore. He'll have you with him in the garden, learning to become an expert at the rows. I can picture you following him as he cultivates with his hand plow. He says you were our best crop of all in 1973. You make our love even more complete.

Dear Sarah:

Sundays have a different feeling around here. It's a special day of the week. After church we spread out the Sunday paper and your father puts on records from the Morman Tabernacle Choir. Then we read or perhaps continue our ongoing game of Scrabble. We've been keeping a running score for months now, and it really bothers your father that I am winning! He knows twice as many words as I, and, in addition, I play with a real nonchalance. But still the scores show that I am ahead. We tack our tally sheet to the refrigerator and the winner of the most recent match will often boast and carry on in front of friends. I love the compassionate, lighthearted rivalry of our contests.

But it is clearly only in the game of Scrabble that I have a chance. When your aunts and I engage your daddy in any type of a factual question-and-answer game we are all losers before we begin. Your father's recall of any learned data is instant and complete. He retains the detail of fourteenth-century English history the way I have retained only my dress size and name! He is unbeatable.

Still, we all enjoy one another and have shared many a long afternoon. I wait for the day when you will also be an integral part of our fun. Right now your father watches you as you wiggle around the floor. He smiles quietly and coaxes you with a toy. How we enjoy our simple days and your growing love!

Dear Sarah:

I'm sitting here at the living room window, watching the speck of your hat disappear down the street atop your father's backpack. My heart wrenches a little that you have already grown so independent of me. Yet your love fills me and makes me glad.

Did you like that treat last night? Payday. And feeling rich with his extra change, your father came home with his pockets stuffed with tootsie pops. We laughed and happily argued for first choice of flavor. Next year you'll join in.

AUGUST, 1974

Dear Sarah:

What heat! Outside is hot. Inside is hotter. I am amazed
that you don't complain. We have all sorts of fans going,
but this old house seems designed to breed heat. There's
nothing cool to circulate.

Even in the heat, your father walks out to check the
garden. We've used no fertilizer or insecticides, but even
so, it prospers. He says that God has spread his hand
over it and thus we'll have his good bounty.

Dear Sarah:

I never thought of myself in a kitchen somewhere, part of the community of mothers everywhere who wash breakfast dishes to the sounds of Captain Kangaroo. But here I am—part of the ranks. How you love the cartoon segments! You delight in dancing in fantasy with Dancing Bear. You are so full of wonder at everything new. And there will be a world to show you. It's exciting.

Your father found some swordfish at a market in Meriden last night. It was $4 a pound, so he surprised me with three quarters of a pound, and we savored every bite! The treat was partly to cheer me up after a bad day—one of my real winners. In my usual rush I grabbed blindly for a detergent bottle and washed all our clothes with Mop 'n' Glo. I wonder if I will *ever* change?

Dear Sarah:

In two days you'll be one year old.

Watching you unfold this year has been the prize for every hard thing I've ever done. How easily I can now overlook those first exhausting days (and nights!). Such memories: our winter walks with the carriage, with only your nub of a nose peeking through the soft stack of blankets; the way you decorated our house with Cheerios (Cheerios Forever!); watching you swim at the Y, somehow trusting you to bob to the surface of the water; and the books.

You and your books. We have read books endlessly, you and I. The same stories, over and over again. Your father shakes his head at my patience with you. Patience I usually lack, but if you ask, I read the same story five times in a row. And if you hold up the book again, I start in for number six. I'm not sure why. Just something in my heart says that in "the whole of my life" I may not always be able to meet your wishes so easily. But today you're little and it's simple. I know what you'd like and the supper dishes will wait. We'll read your story again.

So yes, Sarah, I mean it when I sing to you that "You're My Best Girl." Even when you jiggle your musical Bumble Bee at 6 A.M. and wake me up, I still overflow loving you.

Happy, Happy Birthday, Number One.

Dear Sarah:

I ache today, but it's not from doing chores. My sore
knee was earned from continually bending down to
"kiss better" all your bumps and bruises. The more you
learn to do, the greater the number of accidents seems to
grow. But what a thrill to experience your little steps.
"Out on my own, Mommy! Here I go!"

Then, just like me, you invariably trip over something and hit your head. Your father laughs and sighs
that he'll have two nuts on his hands now.

Dear Sarah:

It's quiet in the house tonight. Your father is studying and writing, and you are far into your dreams. Later your daddy and I will sit and discuss the ideas he's considering for chapters on his thesis about Tolstoy.

It's funny how differently we approach things. I am always wondering about people—what inspires them, what moves them, what causes them to hate and love. But your father relates their actions to *all* life and history, to the development of the systems of thought he has studied. Together our view is that much wider. And I like it that we share our different perceptions. I hope we'll always sit up talking.

Dear Sarah:

What is it that so fascinates you about clocks? Your
aunts were visiting us this weekend and we laughed at
the way you go crazy when you see one, especially one
that chimes. I bet I have spent eight hundred hours listening to you exclaim, "Look! Clock!" over and over,
and then watching you scrutinize the pendulum if we
were lucky enough to find a Grandfather.

You and your daddy had a good walk to Taft School
today. It has to be bitterly cold for us to miss your walk
there. He said that you spent quite some time trying to
get away from your shadow. Knowing him, he cheered
you on!

Dear Sarah:

Will you ever wonder what you were like when you were sixteen months old? Well, today we danced magnificently before the stereo, laughing ourselves into one another and ending up louder than the music. Then we walked so far at Taft School, playing so many games of peek-a-boo in the bushes, that you needed a "pick-up" before we were halfway home.

And now, each night before you go to sleep, I hold you on my lap in the rocker and sing "Rock-A-Bye Baby." You'll never know how I feel, your curly head on my chest, as I hear you softly join in at the end of the lullaby. Your little notes hug the night air and are sweet far beyond my remembering them.

Dear Sarah:

Today you were an imp. I'm trying so hard to sew you an Easter coat and bonnet, but when I piece something together and want you to try it on, you smile and call, "Pretty, Mommy," and then fly away! You leave the material flapping and I can't even adjust one pin. I get so frustrated. You'll be the only child in church wearing bias tape and uncut wool!

But though I tried, I couldn't be stern. I ended up laughing with you. I can easily forget, but then you remind me: no coat is really all that important. We'll do it some other day.

Every day is fun for us. You pore over your books yourself when I'm busy, and when I sew, you quietly sort your own basket of ribbons and tape measures and such. When we play we laugh heartily and smile like conspirators at things only we would know. I like the way we understand one another.

Dear Sarah:

For someone with very dark Italian looks, and only one quarter Irish blood, you surely were festive for St. Patrick's Day. I thought your green overalls and a tiny shamrock were a nice enough gesture to the day. But *you* went on to spill a full jar of green "sprinkles" for cookie decoration all over the kitchen floor. Believe me, when I saw the mess I celebrated too, and cried!

We spend so much time in our kitchen. It's fun to cook for your father because there is nothing he doesn't eat and love. Mealtime here is notably special. And we doubly love this house with lots of friends around the table. Our many friends are a real blessing.

Your father is already looking forward to our new garden. We've been out raking, clearing leaves and debris. Even you spend more time in the yard, now that you're bigger. This year your father says that the garden will be a family effort.

Dear Sarah:

Not that you'll really care, but constant repairs are forcing us to sell my beloved VW convertible. Funny, for you will never remember it, even though that's how we went to the hospital for you and how we proudly brought you home. It will only be part of a story I'll tell you someday.

I must be going soft, sitting here thinking nostalgically about my car. Do you think it's the sickness? I've had awful stomach flu and haven't even gotten up to care for you in two days. That feels so funny. I am so used to being responsible for you that it is a struggle to watch your father take over completely. Sometimes I lie here, laughing at your voices. I'm sure the kitchen looks fire-bombed, and your shirt and pants haven't matched yet. But I hear you two chatting along, coming up with some kind of nourishment three times a day—and running something that sounds like the washer. Your father has voiced not a word of distress, but I do notice how he dives for the bed shortly after you go to sleep. And I'm here, almost viewing my own life—sort of stepping back to take a look at us. Secretly, the rest feels nice. And we look good.

Dear Sarah:

Your daddy's busy with school work so much these days. Writing this thesis on Tolstoy is so important to him. It's become much more than just an academic paper required for his advanced degree. He's really grown to love the man, having spent so much time questioning and considering his ideas. At night we continue to talk together about his novels. It's so hard to find your own set of values—your own philosophy.

In the daytime, while your father reads and studies, you and I play a game of "Mice." How quiet can we be so that daddy has a chance to read and think?

Still, he caught us going out for our walk this morning. "No," he said, he couldn't come along—"too much to do." And yet before we had left the yard he'd taken my hand and joined us. He never said why he changed his mind. And I didn't have to ask. I'd seen him watch us. And probably from somewhere our old promise had surfaced: that we wouldn't forget that we didn't need to be rich or important or revered. But we did need to be together. We said that if family didn't come first most of the time, then we'd lose it. You have to work at family.

Will we always be so fortunate, to remember that promise? It's so easy to lose to countless temptations. I pray for us.

Dear Sarah:

Now we know for sure that we live in *Water*town. What
flooding we are experiencing! We've shed many tears
over our garden. So many plants were devastated, and
the existing squash are rotting from mold. That culvert
which runs beneath our garden has flooded everything.
And it's an irony when you think of it. For previously it
supplied the secret trickle of water which has been the
heart of our plentiful harvests. But today the culvert
worked for ill. And the teeming rains have beaten plant
after plant into the ground. We will still harvest, yes. But
the garden will not bear this time as well as we know it
can.

I think we almost feel hurt by nature, although your
father is much more receptive than I. He accepts the
natural process. Listen to what he put in his Garden
Journal: "These are conditions beyond a man's control.
Wisdom lies in working earnestly and thoroughly and
not in anguishing over creation's design."

For me, that can be so hard. Even tonight we sat up
late talking about Greg, your little friend who's been
running a very high fever. I told your father that I didn't

know how Greg's parents stood it. If *you* were that sick, I *couldn't* stand it. How would I understand nature? I have all that I can do to write the thought. I fear I fall short of trustingly accepting what I cannot control.

Dear Sarah:

We're visiting your Grandma and Grandpa in Massachusetts for a few days. You've told them the secret that has
us so excited: "Mommy's having a baby." Our family of
three—about to be four. Life is so good!

True, we never have an extra penny. Sometimes I
wonder if we'll be able to pay all the bills. We fear that
unexpected expense. But your daddy reads to us from
the Bible. And when I'm sad he reads me poetry. And so
the moments of worrying pass. We work hard in our garden and I make our clothes, our cereal and our bread.
Our life is rich in another sense.

And when we undertake anything—from a big trip
to a new day, we sit down together first to say a prayer.
We never seem to wind up with any extra, but the ends
always meet. I think we're blessed. God watches over us.

Dear Sarah:

This summer is bringing such special moments. We walk together every morning, exploring the grass, bending over to look for flowers. I feel so good. One new child is beginning within me. And you, our first child, are growing in love. We watch with pride as you learn and accomplish so many things. You thrill your father, clad in your Oshkosh overalls, running down the garden rows calling out, "Tomatoes, celery, lettuce . . ." We never imagined a little girl who'd know and love our garden too.

I laugh at the hushed way you excitedly whisper, "Cherries!" when you peek into the bag I bring home from the store. Or the way you eat ice cream by biting the middle of the cone first. And who else would sell all her worldly goods for a bowl of chocolate pudding?

We hadn't planned to do it, but we're going to take you to Massachusetts again for a few days. It's so hot, and we want you to see the ocean. You, who are thrilled by the tiniest treasure. Whatever will you think of the great sea?

Dear Sarah:

We were driving home from Grandma's. You must have
been full of memories of the sand, and the endless holes
you and daddy filled with the sea. Such good days, but
going home always feels best. I was queasy with morning sickness. Your daddy reached over and squeezed
my hand. Almost there. You squirmed. I asked,
"Would you like a cookie?" and as I turned around to
reach your hand all I knew was a white car driving at
us. My God.

And now, just like nothing, just like the earth, in a
second, can be *not* the earth, they are telling me, "I'm so
sorry." I'm looking into eyes full of pity and concern. I
hear my voice giving phone numbers, telling names,
reassuring strangers that I'm all right.

My act must be good. They whisper, "She's so
brave." My mouth goes right along. I tell them not to
worry about me. "Don't x-ray," I say, "I'm pregnant."
Why is my mouth so composed? Roy and Sarah are
badly hurt. Roy and Sarah are dying.

Something hard is happening inside of me. This *has*
to be a dream. How can I make it a dream? Are you

kidding? This can't be my life. Make it go away. It's a joke. Horror like this can't find room inside of me. I don't believe a thing.

Dear Sarah:

This dream is still going on. It won't quit. Time keeps passing, with or without me. I've stopped inside, but the outside of me refuses to recognize that everything has gone wrong. Just like any other Monday, any other Tuesday, they bring me three meals a day. They go on with their lives. They think the world is functioning. And I can't take charge to stop them. I can't even stop me. I'm lost to myself.

You in another hospital. You, without me, dying. It cannot get inside of me and become reality. I cry, but they are not my tears. I'm no longer me. I'm so far lost. How could this happen? Who can stop it? It has got to be stopped. Every muscle and vein in my body is screeching. Can't they hear me? This is happening to me and I can't stop it. I can't make it go away. It keeps going on in spite of me. How could this happen?

Dear Sarah:

"Do you understand?" they say. They say, "This is so difficult to ask—but if she *did* die, would you want her kidneys to be. . . ." I can't even believe it. Why am I a patient in this room with these people in this room saying these things to me? I'm just about insane and they're asking me for philosophy.

I won't answer anyone. They'll have to go away.

Dear Sarah:

I fell apart a bit but it's okay now. You'll recover. You'll
see. It's just a matter of getting through these bad days.
And I'll help you. I'll help you in every way I can. We'll
be out of these hospitals soon.

Now I'm asking those questions which have scared
me. "Will she have to learn to walk again?" Don't worry.
I've read about it in magazines. We'll laugh one day that
it seemed like such a big deal. "Have they cut off her
curls for the surgery?" My little head. But forget it, because hair grows.

So you see, we're all right. Just that they've got you
apart from your daddy and me. I can't understand how
that could happen, because we're always together. How
is life allowing this? But not for long. Your daddy's
coma will lift, and he'll help me care for you. We're a
family.

Won't somebody go to you and tell you two I love
you?

Dear Sarah:

They said it's over. They said Sarah died this morning. What do they mean, "Sarah died this morning?" As if you were some separate person from me. You don't die. *You just don't die.* You don't die without me dying too. Your father will go crazy. He'll wake up from the coma and go crazy. We won't be able to go on. I cannot even believe that this is my life. It's like a play that won't leave, or stop.

Dear Sarah:

I can't care. I can't care any more what they come in here and say. The feeling is gone. They've beaten me. They've won. They said that your father died. He's dead. Daddy's dead too. They have ripped my whole world. There is no more truth to come. They can't say anything else to me. Are they glad? Are they satisfied?

I knew that your daddy had died. I knew. I knew before they came with their words. I heard him going. But I couldn't stop him.

Why has God done this? I can't believe it. Why would he take you both and leave me here? Why didn't I die too? I don't want this life. You two are my life. I just want to die too. How could this happen?

Dear Sarah:

Wasn't I good enough to die with you? Am I being punished? I know I am. So many times I've been foolish, and not really loving—and now I'll pay. You died because you were mine and I wasn't good. But how could a good God be so mean?

I should be back in our garden, or making custards for supper. But I'm in this hospital, sending for relatives to get your burial clothes. I'm talking about caskets. I'm telling everyone that it's all right. It's *not* all right. Why did you die? You were only a baby. At least sadness can never find you now. I'd never want you to know this.

Dear Sarah:

Where are you? Are you and your daddy together? Why have you left me here alone like this? How could this happen?

What is it like where you are? Is it really better? How could you two know and not tell me? I feel so powerless against this terrible mistake: I've been left behind. We go everywhere together, but you two have chucked me away. I can't change this. How will I bear it?

Your daddy used to tease me because I'd take life so seriously. I was always meeting people and seeing through them, feeling their hurts and their sadness. I wanted to share with them our feelings of happiness, but was never really sure how. And your father would make me laugh at my own intensity. He'd say, "Life is not easy for you, Paula!" Well what would he say now? I'll never be the same.

Dear Sarah:

There are constantly people around, and I want to be
alone. I've moved in with your grandparents in Massachusetts because everybody said I should. I left our
home, our dear rooms, our garden. Everybody said that
I couldn't stay there now. So I did what they said to do.
That's what I do now.

But it's still awful here. I'm in my old room with my
old things—but it's not my home. I'm not at all who I
was when I used to live here. I'm not who I was one
month ago. I have a memory of that person. But I don't
know how to get her back.

I was so good to you, and I loved you so. Why did
you leave me?

Dear Sarah:

I can't be polite to one more visitor. No one would like
me if they knew what I really was thinking when they
say how lucky I am that I wasn't badly injured. That I
lived. The person I used to be would have understood
their intentions. What *do* you say to me?

But today I can't pass off the words. This new person doesn't have energy left to do anything but stay
alive and not scream. I don't want to hear anyone else's
awkward attempts. They make me angrier than I
already am.

Dear Sarah:

My only consolation is that I have no regrets. I couldn't have loved you two any more. Only that makes losing you imaginable. I've blown lots of things in my life, but thank God I realized what I had when I had you. I just never realized that you could leave.

I want to talk about you. It's all that's on my mind. I've got to say it over and over again. I still can't believe it. How could this happen?

I make everyone feel so uncomfortable. No one knows how to treat me. I hid in a store aisle today rather than see an old friend and watch her get awkward. I'm always afraid I'll see someone I know and they'll have to say they're sorry. I'll never be known for me again. My face enters a room and I hear everyone thinking— *the tragedy.*

Dear Sarah:

Why won't everyone stop trying to protect me? Or stop trying to be so anxiously nice? I want to take care of my own life. (But I don't know how. Will I ever make a decision again? What did I lose that my mind won't work?) Why do I do what anyone says? Did God inflict this sorrow? Is he angry with me? Did I live through this for some reason? My mind is so troubled with questions.

I went home to Connecticut last week, and friends and family helped me to empty out our house. It was like tearing down everything we'd built and denying that it once was there. It packed us away as if we'd never happened.

I look at your clothes and your father's clothes. It's all over now. The worries, the cares, the events, the occasions. One day it all ends in clothes and shoes, deserted in a closet. They make the worries and ambitions seem so silly. They laugh out loud at everything superficial that we let matter. Because one day everyone's clothes will hang alone in the closet. And so what was it all for?

If we fuss about our lives—if we make clothes and houses and work and events of great importance, then

in the end we'll get fooled. In the end they are so tempo-
rary. There was to be something more. But I missed it. I
counted on tomorrow and I counted on the two of you. I
easily put off the question of what really matters, of
what gives life meaning, of what is directing my life. Always so busy.

And now here I am—with plenty of time—fingering
your father's bathrobe and holding your stuffed Bumble
Bee. I'll keep them both in my closet. I want to remember what gets left behind until I can find that *something*
which doesn't.

Dear Sarah:

While I was in Connecticut I saw Dr. Audet, the doctor who delivered you. There was so much I wanted to say, but tears kept finding my throat. He was like proof to me that I hadn't made the rest of my life up. He remembered that you were true.

I asked him to transfer my records to Massachusetts and my new life: the outline of you and your father and all my joy, reduced to an office card and mailed off in a manila envelope. Mailing off what once was.

He was willing to comply, but gently suggested that he mail only a copy. "Then if you ever choose to return, I'll still have all my data right here." The thought brings tears again, because I do so want him to deliver this new baby. No one will ever know. But that doesn't matter because I've been moved. And so I can't come back. I could have copies of my files all over the world, but I've been moved.

Dear Sarah:

Look at these letters. I can't believe the hundreds of
cards and notes that have arrived, that keep coming.
How I am blessed, all around, with love. Special friends,
like Judy, say they feel far away, but they really are quite
near. They can't imagine how strongly I feel them, and
their love.

Students write, and one told that your daddy
"helped show *myself* to me. . . ." Others tell how often he
spoke of you and me in his classes, of how he said that
his family meant more to him than life itself, that he
would have chosen nothing different in his life than our
marriage and your birth.

I watched your father look at you so many times. He
had a very special smile for you, Sarah. How he de-
lighted in you and in our love. Is he taking care of you
still? I often cry, "Why aren't you here, Roy, to help me
bear this sorrow? Why am I alone? Why have you both
gone at once?" And though that is true—*both gone*—I
cannot follow that thought for very long, for it leads to
the horrible space where your father once was.

Your father is gone too. I can say that he is gone. I can tell someone that Roy died. But I can't really face the pain beyond the words. I can hardly think of that now. It is there, but I have to push it away, for I am almost overwhelmed just by trying to face *your* being gone. Other realities will have to wait for their time.

Dear Sarah:

Tonight I stood outside Nell and Bill Judge's door. Surprise! Yes, it's really me! I'm back home in Connecticut—well, for a little while. Back for some days of visiting . . . of remembering . . . of trying to make that life which used to be mine seem real. As if it *did* happen.

How good it felt to be in their home those few hours, to be welcomed, as I needed to be, to talk with their daughter, Nancy, the babysitter whom you loved so well. The evening let me pretend that I was whole again, able to live on my own. I tried on the life that used to be mine.

In the preceding two days I'd been all over town. I rushed to see Dona. I had supper with the Maxwells. I visited John and Linda and talked for hours with dear Glenna and Bob. I wanted to know about the wedding plans between Pat and Katie. I looked up Abe. I telephoned Jean. I felt great energy, and I went on and on and on.

But ultimately even I couldn't be fooled. I grew suddenly very tired. I made such an effort again at the

Judge's door. If they could only infuse me with their strong love.

But it could not work, my brief masquerade, for I hadn't the strength to sustain it. I will drive back to Massachusetts tomorrow, and now I am very sad. Their lives have all gone on, and mine is still blown apart. I cannot find me. I am a name from a memory.

Dear Sarah:

Days and days and days go on. I'm here going through all the motions, but I'm not really here. I know I act almost right, but I'm not right. I'm not fooled at all. I can never forget, not even to sleep. I think I'll never sleep. Never ever again.

And then when a moment of sleep does come it's no relief but only more pain. Dreams of you and your father and this horror. Does this go on forever?

Dear Sarah:

Halloween. But there is no mask in the world which can hide me from this nightmare. I wish there were.

I was thinking today about Dr. Audet. So many weeks have passed since I saw him last. But some of his words are just now repeating loudly in my head. "If you ever choose to return. . . ." I start, and I can't believe it. This is honestly the first time that it has occurred to me that I do have a choice. I mean, I can go back to Connecticut if I want to! *I can go anywhere I want to.*

I have choices. I can decide. My life is still up to me. How could I not know that? Where have I been? How do I get myself back?

Dear Sarah:

I thought this pain would leave when I remembered
that I had choices. But choices make it worse than ever.
Choices don't help at all, because this new person
doesn't know *how* to make choices. This new person has
no skills at all.

I'm sitting here with this open notebook, facing a
page with a line drawn down the middle. Left side:
"Pro—Move back to Connecticut." Right side: "Con—
Stay here." I have to write all the thoughts down because I can't hold ideas in my head anymore. You and
your father are all I hold in my head. And trying to
make this decision is making me crazy. It's too hard.
Making up my mind is too hard for me. But I'm not like
this. Or I wasn't. How can I not know what I want?

Why do you suppose I am alive? Will I find out? My
life just makes no sense. I am flooded with questions
without answers. My mind will never be still. Always
Roy and Sarah. Roy and Sarah. That's all I know.

When someone talks I can't really listen. Never before have I been unable or unwilling to lend an ear to another's troubles. But I can't anymore. I'm a madwoman

inside. I'm so saturated with hurt and questions that there's no room for anybody else. There's hardly room for me. How could this happen to me? When will it stop?

Dear Sarah:

Day after day I fill out insurance forms. I sort through carton loads of your father's papers. It's not fair that I've been left with all of this. I ought to be making you a quilt for the winter, not sorting the boxes of papers piled in this lousy garage. Every paper, every scrapbook, every memento of us hurts me. What would our life be like today if you were both alive? What would we be busy with? Might I be sitting in our living room taking you both for granted, never guessing that this could happen?

Everyone asks me about the court decision and about the man who killed you. They hope that there will be a big settlement. They want to see him punished. And what if he is? What if he is tortured? What if his loss makes me rich? Neither money nor revenge will bring you back. There is no victory for me in a court.

All I'd like is to sleep again. Will I ever stop having nightmares? At night my mind makes me face what I don't want to face: you will never be back.

I still need to talk. I still have to say it again and again. "We were in a terrible accident and Roy and Sarah were killed." Sometimes I catch myself blurting it out to strangers. I guess in a way that's easier. I can say it, and a stranger doesn't try to take my pain. I want to hide my feelings from anyone who knows me.

Can you understand that? You see, my feelings are the only things I have left which haven't been wrested from me. My tears and my pain over you are all I still have which belong to the three of us.

Everything else is gone. So even if it does hurt, it's the last thing I have which is ours. Everything else in my life is new—something you're not a part of. I hope you can see that. These tears are all that's left of us.

Dear Sarah,

It is bleak today—bleak and bitterly cold. The day is me.
I hate the way I am angry. I dislike my pain which
strikes out at everyone. I saw a bouquet of flowers at the
store this morning and bought them for my mother. I
feel like I'm so mean to her, as if she receives my anger
just because she's the one who's most often there. I'd
like the flowers to erase who I am and don't want to be.
They say, "I'm sorry."

People are better to me than I deserve. My sister
Anne gave up her room so that I could be where I was
when I used to live at home; my sister Bev tirelessly
makes trips anywhere I want to go; her twin, Barby, en-
courages me endlessly to visit, to come for supper, to
join her and her husband at a movie, a play; my grandmother says again and again, "Is there anything I can
do?"; and the dear neighbors I call Grandma and Grandpa
Wild, themselves sick, visit me every single day.

It is nearly a visible support, this circle of love. With
the help of my friend David and your Uncle Jim I pack
away many of your father's papers and deliver cartons
of his books to libraries or churches. My dear cousin

Nancy drives all the way from Narragansett every week because she knows I need someone here. Once we laughed through Europe together, thinking a crisis in life was which boy on the tour to date. Now we eat lunch together on the piers in Newport, wishing the sea might tell us what in life allows such pain. And again and again Betty, my oldest friend, calls. She listens to me talk on and on. I repeat the words about you and your father and our lives. I talk about going on. I try to make my life make sense. But it does not make sense. And I do not talk about the pain I feel, and the love. I hold that within me. That is ours.

These loving people most likely do not know it, but right now they are the structure which causes my life to go on. They have become *me*, for a little while, and they carry on my days until I can catch up with it all. *If* I catch up. Do any of them notice that I am gone? I am not even here.

Dear Sarah:

There's a new television program on, and you don't know it. I read something in the newspaper which would interest your father, and I can't tell him. He'll never know. Every day new things happen and I know, but you don't. How can this be so? How can you be really gone? Who can I tell the things I shared only with your father? Who takes care of me? Who even needs me?

I'm looking at things so differently now. I used to be so sure of my future. I was always planning for that future. And now your father's words repeat in my head and haunt me: "Life has no guarantees." There is no guarantee of anything more than the moment we have. So if we don't use "today" well, then we've got ourselves fooled.

Just think of your father. He was only 33 years old, but he'd asked himself so many important questions about life. He wondered about ultimate truth. He sat every day with the Bible, looking for deeper understanding. He controlled his life. He didn't let himself get caught up in petty tales and gossip; he didn't let himself rush around so much that a day had no time for prayer or reading.

And what if he *had* thought that he would take time for God later, when he was in his forties or fifties, when his family was settled, and it was easier to slow his life down? Then it would have been too late. The only important questions about life would not yet have been asked, and he would have died. Who would believe that 33 years could be too late? That's our great delusion.

Dear Sarah:

I get afraid I'll never know where I'm heading again.
Will I ever be a nice person again? I used to do so much
listening, but that's gone. I'm so full of wanting you that
there's no room inside of me for anybody else. I can't
take anything else in. When will this stop?

Dear Sarah:

Today did it. I cannot take one more day of everything being upside down. A new obstetrician, a new pediatrician, new stores, new banks, new pharmacies. Every simple thing I need to do means asking directions or looking things up. The outside of my life has become as strange as the inside of me. How I ache for something to be familiar.

And there I was today, crying in the aisle of the store because I couldn't find the peanut butter, and then I knew. I'm getting out of here. I'm going home.

Dear Sarah:

My swollen belly and I are wedged onto a crate, super-
vising as they move all of our memories into this new
apartment. These particular rooms are new, but the land
is home, the streets are home, my friends are home and
my dear doctor is here. And yes, God, if I go down to
the First National store, I'll know just where to find the
peanut butter. That has become my victory. I must be a
crazy woman.

Where would we all be now if the accident had
never taken place? What would we be like? Could we
possibly just be living normal days, never guessing that
one blink of fate was separating us from this madness I
know?

Do you notice that I never write to you about this
baby? Maybe when my body is at rest in this place I can
finally turn my mind to him. I know I've been unfair. I
haven't loved and enjoyed his stay here like I did yours.
I don't even know if I'm able to love someone new. But
nature is keeping its own timetable, regardless of my
consent. And what if I do want this baby and he dies
too? Do you see?

But my time is running out. Soon I'll have to face all the possibilities. I even wonder what my sobbing is doing to this child. I am so sorry. But I'm too exhausted to make things different. All my energy goes into not screaming, screaming forever. There isn't any strength left over for wanting someone new.

DECEMBER, 1975

Dear Sarah:

Here I am. But how was the energy ever found—the strength to make this move? What enabled me to come back here to Connecticut and start again? The pain of choosing to return was its own nightmare. Yet once resolved, it only became the pain of saying to my family, who has shown me so much love and care, that now I must go off again on my own.

I will ever remember the afternoon I sat in the living room with your grandpa, telling him that I was going to leave. It hurt me to look into all of his love and not be able to stay. But I knew I had to do this, for me.

There were fears that he had. He knew that life could change and be cruel, that I might return to a memory and find it wasn't there. His most natural impulse was to keep me from harm's way. But what he *would* do, and what he did, were gratefully not the same. Protection might have insisted—pleaded—that I stay; instead, love trusted me out into the storm. If ever I needed his love it was in that hour. I needed support for the step I was desperately taking against my own fear. And he stood behind me, and let go.

He looked at me quietly and said, "I hope it will all be well." His look was deep, and our strongest emotions were there. Then we were silent for a long, long time. I wanted to hug him, I wanted to cry. I wanted always to be his little girl. But my feelings were too strong, and I fought their expression. If I gave into them, maybe I wouldn't be able to go. And going was right. And so it ended that there wasn't any more we could say.

Eventually I left to make some arrangements and to begin packing some things in my room. And your grandpa sat for a while longer in his chair. Then he left, too. And that night I cried, alone, knowing that I had caused him the pain of that goodbye. I never meant it to be so.

On the morning that I actually left I had to avoid eveyone's eyes. I said, "Well, you're rid of me. This is it!" Did I sound brave? For them, I hope so. For in reality I had only the strength to shut the car door and pray to God I could last the three hours of my journey. I was only sure of strength to get from one minute to the next. And I saw every mile of the road through aching tears. I wept without clear thought of what I was weeping for. I simply wept, exhausted and lost. I drove on because that's what I had decided to do. I could not resurrect and debate that choice. There was only energy given to meet it once.

And so I drove through tears. I wondered what would be the particular face of the storm. And finally I looked up to see that I had arrived, by a miracle, at my new home.

Dear Sarah:

I look at these boxes that I haven't the energy to unpack. Look at me. This has really happened to me. I'm hanging on to sanity by a thread. My mind holds a madwoman who can't be shut off. I can't forget. I see people taking things for granted, and I'm so angry with them without wanting to be.

Isn't there some way of knowing what I know without having to go where I've been?

But how can I be exasperated with anyone else? Am I any different? Did I ever value each day? Did I ever ask myself what in life had lasting meaning, and then live as though that mattered? I used to treasure wholesome things, or so I thought. I felt I had important goals: raising you, loving our family, extending myself to others. I put my love for those things first in my life. And my heart never saw then that it all wasn't permanent. Even those good things, when put first, don't answer what moves the universe and didn't sustain me when you were gone.

Dear Sarah:

Christmas. The Son of God was born. God who moves
the world; who is the only thing which hasn't moved.
That God who loved the world. And in this moment of
quiet it occurs to me that he loves me. I am part of the
world. Where has that thought come from? But it persists. He never guaranteed anything to be permanent ex-
cept his Love. I made all the other conclusions.

I feel some rest. For a time I'm thinking about Mary
and Bethlehem. I've lost all that I held most dear, and
yet my life need not lose its meaning. Something says
sorrow would have me were it not for Bethlehem.

Dear Sarah:

A new year. But I don't want anything new. I want us back together again. My mind is getting louder and louder. What if we hadn't stopped for a few minutes at that gas station? What if I hadn't been handing you a cookie and you hadn't been reaching forward? Did it *have* to be? Was this some nonerasable destiny? That question won't stop asking itself.

Who or what made these circumstances that I haven't made? Did you die so young to fulfill some mysterious purpose? What purpose? Does God direct every breath of our lives, and so we are powerless victims? Or do we control our lives and thus we controlled the circumstances which put us in just that spot on the road at the wrong time? If I don't go mad from sorrow, I'll go mad asking these questions.

Dear Sarah:

Where are you? Is there really life after death? Before, that was a neat rhetorical question. Now it's an over- whelming enemy. If I could know for sure, maybe it would ease this tormenting chest pain. Who would be- lieve that grief could actually be physical? But the pain is real. It says that you were alive one minute, and then I never saw you again. You see, I'm not writing a story. I'm talking about *you*. My baby.

Were you scared in that hospital? Did you think I'd deserted you? I suffer thinking that you might have be- lieved that, that you might have wanted me and thought "Mommy!" but I wasn't there. I cannot stand that thought.

The most horrible voice deep inside of me thinks that you don't love me anymore. Otherwise why would you and your father have gone off together and left me like this?

These thoughts keep coming upon me, and I can't stand their pain. Why is this happening? And why now? Shouldn't the worst have been over many, many months ago? They all talked about shock. Could I have been in shock for months? Is that possible? It was bad then, but never like this. Have I really been protected all this time and now the shelter is slipping away? Can I get it back? I'm scared. What do I do? I will never make it through day after day of this. I'm seeing and feeling what I don't want to know. I'm looking straight into that horrible space between us, and I will never make it.

Do you think if I just let go and cry it all out then one day the tears will stop? What if I never stop crying? They're all out there telling one another that I have such courage. And here I am—so very, very scared.

In September someone sent me a booklet of Norman Vincent Peale's and I read it over for the second time today. He said that with the help of God nothing can ever destroy or defeat you. That is the only hope I have. All I've got left is a prayer that what he said is true.

Dear Sarah:

I'm still pretending for others. How I wish I could pretend for myself. Just when I felt myself beginning to do well, I'm falling apart. But at least no one knows. When I have to go out, I get all dressed up and I smile. I think I do well. The worse I feel, the better I try to perform in public.

I'm not trying to be dishonest. I just don't want to let anyone know how badly off I am. You are *my* loves, and this is *my* grief. And I do think I've got almost everyone fooled. They think my mourning is over now. They figure enough time has passed . . . and I don't blame them. I used to think grief went away quickly too.

They try so hard to "involve" me again. They're inviting me here and there. They look at my face and they assume it's me. They feel that I can do things again. They're ready for me to be well. But their conversations, their attempts, are all bouncing off this crazy mind. I'm not me. I'm cracking up.

Day after day I take the phone off the hook, lock my door and cry. Hour upon hour the tears come. I want you, I need you, and I can't get over it. I can't accept it.

It's this despair of being left. It's this incredible chest pain which says I can't have my baby or my husband. Me moaning? Wasn't I too controlled for that? But I've lost those controls. I'm just crying and crying and crying.

I'd give anything. I'd accept you ill and nurse you for a hundred years. I'd take you in an endless coma. I'd even see you and then leave you again. *But just to see you once more.*

Dear Sarah:

"You're so brave." How many times will someone tell me that I'm so brave? I stand at the window watching the snow fall. Tears wrack my huge belly. I don't want this thought, but it persists: My baby's in that ground. That chilly ground. What if you're cold?

This isn't brave. This is a lady whose mind just won't shut up. I pray and pray to find a way out. But even so I'm cracking up. Maybe it's a good thing that I pretend in public. Those performances are my only relationship to sanity.

Then this baby. My body is preparing to have a baby. And everyone talks about this baby as if it is their answer to my sorrow. But it's not *my* answer. This baby is someone else, and it won't change the fact that you are gone. You are still dead.

My friend Carolyn goes weekly with me to the LaMaze childbirth classes. I feel like such a sight. Everyone else has a husband, as it should be. And then there sit Carolyn and I. It is all wrong. I hate it. "Is this your first child?" they ask. "No, second." "Oh, then how old is your first?" Over and over again.

I am exhausted. I'm so afraid I'll crack up. Life out-side of my mind doesn't even exist for me anymore. You're the only thing that's real, and then sometimes even you seem unreal. Like I dreamed you both. I try and can't remember your faces. That hurts more than everything else.

I'm hardly living "real" life anymore. I'm skimming the surface. I'm alone. My initiative has died with every-thing else. I see that I am loved. That is getting through. I'm blessed with friends and family. I know they're aching to help me, but I can't ask. I can't let them. This pain is ours and not anybody else's. I let go of this and you're gone. Do you see?

Dear Sarah:

How easy it was to have what I called "faith" in our old
life, with our walls full of love and our future full of
promise. How easy, like loving someone who's only gentle and good. But this is hard faith now. I still hear myself praying, but the faith cannot erase the pain. How
hard it is to believe that I am not alone with all this hurt.
How hard it is to believe that there can be a victory the
other side of these tears. But that is Christ's promise.
And I do believe in the power of his words: "Who-
ever . . . does not doubt in his heart, but believes that
what he says will come to pass, it will be done for him"
(Mk.11:23). I pray to find a way out of this. I want to get
through it all.

Dear Sarah:

Something happened yesterday. I am still quite struck. I had dinner with Carolyn's family and tried to chat happily with her children. It was an evening similar to many we have shared. But the following morning their eleven-year-old son, Joe, totally unbidden by any adult, did an incredible thing. He approached Father Jim, the priest for whom he is an altar boy, and asked him to please see a friend of his whom he felt needed some help. Me. That friend was me!

And so the priest has called, and I was so shocked I said yes. Yes, I am going for help. Yes. How could a young child arrange for me what I couldn't do for myself? How could a young child know? I only know that deep within me, I guess I am glad. This pressure of holding on to you has become much too hard. I don't want to go mad. So don't be angry if I talk about us finally. You know I treasure all that we are. But maybe we have to part. I never thought it would come in this way . . . but maybe this is an answer to my prayer.

Dear Sarah:

You—you who've heard everything—you may not believe it, but Father Jim said that the way I am is normal.
All of it. All this craziness—normal. *Normal!* I may not
be a madwoman. In fact, one day I *could* be me again. I
know that right now that's just an idea. But it's such a
strong, positive one.

Do you understand? I could keep having these awful moments of remembering you both, and even think
that I won't live past the pain. And still one day I could
find that it is better. That I'm all right. It's the strongest
hope I've had. I might be me again!

Please don't resent it if I do recover. Don't resent it if
I want this new baby. I think I do. I think I dare to love
again. "We" won't change because of that. Even if I go
on, we will always be a part of me, a memory of our
days together. Nothing touches that. Nothing ever
touches that.

Dear Sarah:

I search through literature and through Scripture. I talk to people. I'm still looking for answers. If only there were easy answers. God loves me. I keep beginning there. And I don't think he watched you riding down the highway and said, "Let's kill her." He loved you too. So then *why?* Why did it happen?

One moment the anger is gone. Then it's back. The pain ceases. It returns. I thought it was possible to reach the saturation point and finally account for all the sadness. But life's not so neat.

Dear Sarah:

My baby is so overdue. I feel tortured, waiting like this. What if the accident damaged him after all? What if he dies, now that I realize that I want him? Could I stand it? Could I love someone else and lose him? I could never stand anyone else dying.

If I didn't need my phone to call the doctor I'd rip it out. I hate it. It rings with everyone's concern. It rings with possibilities I don't want to face. It reminds me how scared I am. Why aren't I me yet? What if I come this close to coming back, and then don't make it all the way?

God, do you ever weep with me? Don't you see the goodness that was thwarted because one man drank too much and hit us with his speeding car and didn't care? Does that man ever think about me, or wonder about Roy and Sarah?

Dear Sarah:

I have lived forever with questions. But slowly some answers are beginning to unfold in my heart. It's no miracle or sudden revelation. But I am beginning to see some things. How I pray to see.

I think part of the *why* our accident happened has to do with all people being free. All of us are free to think and act and make our own choices. And all the choices have consequences—results which fall into the lives of the many others with whom we live. Think of it! And so it was possible that a man drank and raced his car on the highway. His choice. And we were driving home. That choice was ours. And we entered one another's lives in a terrible manner.

Do you see it too? Just one man, motivated by greed or pride or desperation may choose unwisely and jeopardize the good toward which others may have been striving. Man is not perfect. And a free choice may be good or bad. That leaves man with a tremendous potential. A frightening one. That leaves man as a channel of light, or a party to darkness. There's no way *not* to choose.

God did not finger you to die. Rather, nature had its way. Nature and man, neither perfect. But all of us subject to the processes they set in motion. How guilty am I? What have my many thoughtless acts set in motion? How many times have I done nothing and so abetted the darkness? How responsible we are to this life.

And God. Where is he? He changes neither the acts of nature nor of man. We remain free. He created us free, and with that terrible freedom we live. But the moment we prefer the Light, he transforms . . . he transforms not the circumstances, which we create—he transforms *us*.

He transforms how we see what has been there all along. It never changes. We do.

Dear Sarah:

You have a little sister, and I've named her Beth Starr.
Can you see her sleeping here? Do you watch us, and
smile?

Please, God, don't let her die. Don't let my sisters or
parents or anybody die. I couldn't stand it yet. But Beth
is here and safe right now. Hundreds of people have
wished us well, and have perhaps thought that now
things are okay. I wish it were that easy. But Beth is head-
to-toe memories of you. Memories of how your father
and I shared you. And now there's no family. Just me
and a baby. Will I be able to go on?

Only today have I realized that I am not the only
one who grieved. How could I not have known that?
Our friends, our families—so many felt the loss. Your father's parents lost a child too. But it all escaped me. I
have been so far away.

Dear Sarah:

Everyone dies. I mean, no one lives forever. So then why do we live? What is it all for? How easy to focus alternately on either our joys or our tears, as I have done. We get caught measuring life that way.

Your father was right all along. Life is far deeper than one man's particular existence in a given town. How blind I was! History has played out my story against hundreds of backdrops. And though they were important to the individual lives, none of the brief joys and tears have ultimate meaning. Pain would defeat people if it did.

No, all those circumstances around which I measured my life were impermanent. How tempting to believe they were of lasting importance. I acted as if that were so. I let them shape my days. I was easily fooled. They were wonderful and to be cherished only within perspective. As life's final priority, they were false.

All those moments hung one day in the same closet with your empty clothes. The best of them eventually passed. They moved. All that remains, from all that we were, is the love. And Jesus said, "I am the Light of the world." The Light of the world is Love. God, Love, did not move and does not change. So the question in life, every day, for every person, is not what can I enjoy, or who will I please, or how do I look, or what can I do or achieve. The question is, how do I love? Am I a channel for the Light?

I am sure of one thing, my little one. Emptiness is all around us. But if one chooses to look for God, he will not be empty and his life will never be the same. Christ has promised that. And no one avoids that choice, for to ignore it is to decide.

Dear Sarah:

Easter. Look at Calvary. I think I understand it now. Sorrow was even a part of Christ's life. And he didn't remove it because sorrow and joy, together, are facts of our humanness. He knew.

I've feared sorrow and tried to pursue joy. I thought that God ought to prevent all tears. I never realized what it implied when I believed that one's choice is free. God has not sent me these tears. These tears, I finally see, are his same tears from Gethsemane. These tears are man's.

Dear Sarah:

Bit by bit I am able to face the memories, my remembrances of you and your father. I take them out slowly, when I am able, and go over them one at a time. Some moments seem now so distant that they might almost have belonged to another life.

I am sorry that you'll never know me any better, or see me any other way than as a shaky new mother and a young wife. There was more we might have been if your life had gone on. There was more for you to know. I'd like you to have seen me with your father and his proudest purchase, a BMW motorcycle. What trips we took with that bike, the two of us! How I loved my arms about your father, trees and mountains speeding by! What a sense of being free.

I remember the day we climbed the dirt trail that grew too steep. Our beloved bike tipped for the first time, spilling us, rather startled, onto the bumpy ground. We laughed, aching, on the grass—and then righted ourselves and were off again, being from that point on much more respectful of dirt and inclines. We sailed into the wind, passing out the miles to the day, and it seemed that nothing could catch us or harm us. What would?

I dreamed a million dreams, riding along, whispering them onto the lips of the wind. I dreamed us in a thousand different ways. And I hugged your father and loved our freedom and the sun, our flights into spring— our joyful flights. And now the pain that we won't be sailing the highways any longer. The pain bred of love, which was taken away.

One day I longed to pretend that Beth was you, just for one day. Just to have you that one last time. But I couldn't let me do it. You're gone, and it is over.

Then I searched today for our old lawn mower. What did I do with it? I visit friends and see some of our things in their homes. I must have given things away. I don't even remember. I was so far away.

Dear Sarah:

Some days in one's memory are forever vivid, regardless of the passage of time. And I will always know the sounds and will feel and sense every impression that was real to me on the day they said that you had died.

I face that moment today: my friend Carolyn standing there, holding my hand, tears streaming down her face as the doctor spoke. "Your daughter has gone." For a while we stared without thought, Carolyn, just by her presence, holding onto the parts of my life that were now too terrible for me to bear. Then one by one the faces of my family and your daddy's family were all around the bed in that eternal hospital room. Pain lived with us all.

A kindly nurse, with long, dark hair, walked quietly in and out, unsure of how to face my nightmare. There was a gentleness about her. Trays arrived with food. Flowers. Presents which could not erase the way life had reached out to wound. I was never, perhaps, more vulnerable than in those hours . . . and I never felt more betrayed.

Time continued without my knowing or caring that it had. And later in the day I looked up to see Rick, a friend from a time very long ago. Rick had been my close companion in college years, and we'd shared a friendship of a very special kind. He had been a part of my happiest days. We drank beer together, laughed about classes and filled up the emptiness of many long weekends at school. Professors at graduation couldn't believe we weren't to be married, and we grinned that they could have thought so. For ours was not a romance, but a friendship. A unique friendship. Probably a gift.

But years had passed since those carefree days, and now I knew I was not ever to be carefree again. And yet at the precise moment of an agony I couldn't understand, there was the friend I needed. How did he know to come? What impulse prompted him, upon hearing of our crash, to leave work and drive to be at my side?

But the questions come from now. They weren't the thoughts I had then. Then there were no words between us, only tears and his holding my hands . . . my hands which didn't have life. He found my terror and protected me from it, for a while. I was not ready then.

Always that day will include the people and the sounds of those hours. All the life was gone from me, although I could not, as I wanted to, die. Life kept on.

Others were there. And though I could not see it . . . it was true that love was surviving the loss and enduring the pain. From the first terrible moments, I never realized more than I could stand. There was never more than I could bear. Someone, never moving, knew me . . . and did not cease to hold me and care.

Dear Sarah:

What kind of future will I offer Beth? What kind of future will there be for me? I stand by the window watching our neighbors visiting with their families on Sunday. Weekends are no different than weeks for me anymore. Beth and I are so rootless. We don't belong anywhere. I feel like a lady, any lady, living with her baby. Period. Nothing defines us. I walk Beth in her carriage and hate the homes with yards and clotheslines and fathers. There still are moments when I hate my life. It hurts.

But slowly my peace within grows. Can you understand that I still suffer over you and yet I am finding a way beyond it? There is pain and there may always be pain—but it no longer defeats me. I can go on. God's Light transcends human suffering. The hope I clung to is strong and real.

Dear Sarah:

For so long I wished Beth could be you in a thousand different ways. But I've separated you now. I really love her for herself. I think you would love her too. She's very gentle and smiles at little things and seems touched by a special love from all we have come through together.

Don't feel betrayed by our happiness. I love you both. But I don't say any longer, "If Sarah were alive," or "If Roy were here. . . ." You two are gone. Beth and I are the survivors. We go on.

I've held on to you so hard.

Dear Sarah:

I'm doing well. Your deaths are always there, but I'm integrating a lot better now. No more act. No more standing outside of life, looking in. You are always just beyond my conscious thoughts, but I realize that may be so for a long while. Now I can accept that and go on.

I've been thinking. I bet you're longing for the day when I'm completely me again all the time; when I can write to you like I used to, of full and good times. But then it occurs to me that if that day arrives, then there won't be any letter. Or not a letter to you. Do you understand?

Dear Sarah:

I almost bought a house today. When the owner refused my first bid and wanted to negotiate, I came to, with a start. What in the world was I doing? I didn't even like the house, and it was far too much money.

But I knew. It was my last attempt to run. That final desperate chance that if I changed my life fast, and found someplace new, then I still wouldn't have to suffer over you, that I could move away and leave the sorrow.

But this time at least I see hope, because I did eventually catch myself. I caught myself in the same way the "old me" might have done before. I think I'm finally coming around. Somewhere in the near distance I see *me*.

Dear Sarah:

We are all so powerful. You and I and everyone. Our words and our thoughts, which cause our actions, generate so much power in the cosmos. Really, not only the big choices but even the little ones matter—because through all of our choices we set so much in motion. What great waves we generate via our beliefs! Then how important it is that we care about the direction of our lives.

I sat on my porch today feeling lonely. And as my mind wandered, I imagined that I had lived at the time of Christ. How lucky that would have been, I thought. Even loneliness would have seemed easier in his company.

And then it struck me and was so real: Christ *does* live, and we *do* live in the same time. No wishing and no "if only." Christ does live and his Love is here. He alone has never moved. That's the statement of the Resurrection. Nothing dies and nothing ends. When we reach one conclusion we only become part of another beginning. Your father wrote it in his garden log: "Every seed has its Easter." Now, finally, I understand.

Dear Sarah:

I will never be exactly the same, but I know I am ready to go on. Even though our love stretches beyond any grave, my life here is without you. You've become the seed of a new beginning, somewhere I've yet to know. I still cry for you and your daddy, and maybe that will always be so. Some days and some times may always bring tears. I understand and accept that as part of love. But can you see what I'm trying to say? I'm saying good-bye.

Do you remember, from our trip to the ocean, the way the water held the sunlight in the morning? It contained it, and yet never possessed it for its own. I will always hold you as the ocean holds the sunlight. I hold the lullaby we sang together, your voice so little and clear. So say a prayer for me. As I say one for you. And let me go.

Dear Sarah:

I visited you at the cemetery today. Well, not really you, *in fact*, but the you of my heart. I rarely make the trip to that site, for I know you are not to be found there. But still, our last ritual on earth together was the ceremony at that grave.

Now you and your father have journeys I know little of. And when I think of you sometimes, remembering, I visit your ground and leave you violets—a bouquet to the best of our memories, to the moments which will always smile. I think of all that has become of our lives, and though, seemingly, I should feel more fragile, it is only a new strength I am sensing.

I look at what I wrote on your grave marker: "The Lord is My Shepherd, I Shall Not Want." How well I realize now that that is true. Even though, through our free wills, *we* do all the choosing—allowing life and controlling it, overall, is the Hand of the Shepherd. Always, for me, at every moment, he was there—there when I felt his presence, and equally there when it *seemed* I was all alone. His presence did not depend upon my "feeling" it, or even upon the extent of my belief. God was simply there. He did not move, as I realized that first Christmas after losing you.

Also, ironically, neither pain nor happiness were true indicators that he was or was not there, though often I mistakenly thought that too. His purposes work together in *all* conditions of life, if we could only see. Maybe you know all that now. You know much more than I. For even in affliction was love—love even in my tears.

I ached and sorrowed so at losing you. But the pain, in the end, did not have the final say. And so it was all much less a loss than a victory. For Love has the final say—"The Lord is my Shepherd, I shall not want." And we are all quite safe.

EPILOGUE
—Letter to a Friend

Dear Van:

On the 11th of January, 1979, I had a dream that I should like to share with you. I will never know if it was from God. I do know it was startlingly real. I was in some house I cannot place, in the early morning, caring for Beth in the kitchen. I went up to my bedroom to dress, and as I changed I looked up and there was Roy in the hallway, stepping from the bathroom, brushing his teeth. It was so normal, him in his underwear . . . an early morning scene. It was so much he that he began goofing around in a way that was familiar only to us.

My initial thought was, "He's dead . . . how can he be here brushing his teeth?" I never ran to him. We didn't speak. We only motioned and laughed as we did when we expected years and years to stretch before us. I noted that he'd put on weight. At the time of his death he had been lamenting that my cooking was encouraging a pot belly. And I thought to myself, how could he gain weight in heaven? Isn't everything perfect there? He went back to the bathroom and his teeth. I finished dressing, wondering if his naturalness and our remembered joke were meant to convey to me that he was still the same, still essentially Roy—that the personality characteristics weren't diminished or changed. The weight gain? A puzzle.

I went downstairs and sat at the dining room table. Roy came down and went all around the house with tools, checking things out. Finally he came to me and said that he could see that I needed him. There were things to be done that I couldn't do. I asked, "Will you help me?" but he shook his head and said, "I can't." I understood at that point that he was aware of my life . . . but couldn't intervene.

He sat down, then, opposite me at the table. Of all the things I've often said I would ask him if I only had the chance . . . I never said a word. But when he spoke, it was the one thing (I thought afterwards) that I probably needed to hear more than anything else. He told me that he was sorry. That he never intended to leave me. That he loved me, but had had to go. Again I was startled because he was so genuinely sad. I could see that. And I thought to myself, isn't heaven only happy? I thought only the living grieved. But it was clear that it had affected him too, that he had been aware of my pain, but couldn't prevent it. We touched then for the first time—just our hands across the table. I felt aware that we had to be sitting there on borrowed time. But still I never spoke or questioned.

What we did for those few minutes was grieve together over the wreck of our family—the only time my grief was shared. I was so aware of Roy's sense of powerlessness to help me. He said quietly, "At least now you don't have to struggle. You have money." And no sooner had he said the words than I cried and then he did too. The money is the emptiest gain of the whole affair. We sat a while longer with our tears, and then his presence was gone.

I thought to myself, now I'll go back to sleep, and was drifting that way when my telephone rang. The call was from a friend who never calls at 6:50 A.M. and he had no clear reason for the call. An impulse. I was annoyed at first, thinking the dream might have gone on. But having been awakened, I began to write my memories down. Afterwards I wondered if I would ever have recalled it at all if I had not been immediately roused. Who knows?

As I asked at the start, was it merely a dream? Was it a reality? At any rate, I've shared this with you, as I wanted to. And now I am packing up *Song for Sarah* and going off to bed. Thank you for listening to me well into this night.

With love,
Paula

Afterword

Almost twenty years. I open my worn copy of *Song for Sarah* and read it through for the first time since 1985, the ten-year mark. The fall air is clear, and I've just taken a walk around Harvard Square in Cambridge, where I am presently living. As I walked I thought about these memories which have defined so much of my life and shaped my heart.

When this book was first published I pasted pictures throughout the pages of my copy. Now I look at the large color picture of Sarah inside the front cover, taken just before she died. I run my finger over the image of her curls. Sometimes, in speeches, I call the moment of her death my line of demarcation. There is the young woman I was beforehand, with all her hopes and dreams, heart innocent and trusting. Then the crush of cars and the impact of that indefensible moment. A moment that reached out and touched all of my future with its mark. A moment for me when the world became so still. I have never drawn a breath as quiet, or deep. Or that would change so much. A moment which tore apart my small universe. And then there is everything else which has followed . . . the pieces I've put together.

On the title page I find a purple paper flower made by Beth when she was three years old. Underneath it I printed,

Beth's flower. Life goes on.

Such simple words, belying their cost. Or meaning.

Today Beth is eighteen years old, in college, and a blond, blue-eyed beauty. Interestingly, she never asked many questions about her sister and father until she was a pre-teen. She always considered the subject "too sad." Now, as a young adult, she begins to piece together the meaning of her history.

Life wasn't (and isn't) fair. I knew that. But could it still be beautiful? The question haunted me and was at the heart of my years of grieving. I didn't get what I wanted. I got other things. Struggling to unconditionally accept what *was* is perhaps the hardest thing I have ever done.

Since 1980 I have criss-crossed the country meeting others who successfully struggled to say "Yes" to their unchosen circumstances. Together we have shared our heartaches and also our rich discoveries: the need to forego being right; the necesssity of surrendering one's will; the incomparable power of forgiveness; the steadfast, unchanging love of God.

Today I feel as if Sarah and I traded the giving of life. As her mother I gave birth to her physical presence. But through death she gave life to my soul when I learned that I did not own her and could not protect her. It forced me to look at my own life and decide what to do with it. She has been the key to so much truth for me. She and Roy both.

In 1975 I was a young woman and it was a bold, defining heartache. Their deaths made me work so hard at understanding that we are all separate. All God's. No one belongs to anyone else. We only pass through one another's lives. And to do so without controlling, or clinging—to do so only honoring and respecting separateness and differences—changes the landscape. It makes things different. It transforms suffering.

Because of this early tragedy I believe I have lived more mindful of the impact of my choices. I have undoubtedly been more aware of the preciousness of time. I have been loathe to put off opportunities and chances which may never come again. Certainly I have taken more risks and have wholeheartedly given my life's purpose over to the pursuit of God, in all things.

I laugh a little bit (and am glad) at how like Roy I have become over the years. His mind "endlessly searching life for answers." His "pondering what motivates people." His "willingness to learn from the histories of peoples who lived thousands of years ago." His "deep faith." His search for God.

I think of the culvert which ran beneath our garden, causing such flooding and destruction in July, 1975, a month before the world as I knew it ended. Such irony that the secret trickle of water which had been responsible for our previous rich harvests also contained the potential for ruin. Proof that there is nothing inherently good or bad in our circumstances. Nature is. Life is. All things contain the seed of power. It is what God is able to do with our yielded lives ... circumstances ... the water ... our selves, and whether or not we will allow it, that determines how happy we decide to be.

I see clearly today that even the moment of the accident did not hold lasting power. The moment could do nothing without my deciding. The moment actually waited for me. By my choice the moment could confine me or free me. I chose to be free.

Twenty years later something within propels me forward to experience even more beauty and adventure, more of the treasure strewn everywhere by the hand of Love. I see my life as an overwhelming gift. I don't look back. I take all that is behind me, let it speak to my heart as a wise teacher, and only think about the greater joy that lies ahead.

The pain, in the end, did not have the final say. . . .
Love had the final say. And we are all quite safe (p. 108)

We always were. Now, I know.

Paula D'Arcy
November, 1994

YES

Our circumstances are different
Our hurts, hopes and brokenness are different
Many of our fears are different
But our healing journeys,
I realize,
all begin the same way.
With one word.
"Yes."
It is a mystery, like the loaves and fishes . . .
Water into wine . . .
Out of Yes come new beginnings
Yes changes the broken heart
Yes opens the eyes to beauty
Yes moves the suffering, causing it to pass through.
Yes, I will accept the circumstances of my life
I will cry and mourn my losses
Will hold them near until all their wisdom
   has been spilled
Will accept them until God
takes what man meant for evil,
and creates of it a brilliant good.
The very pain that wounded me is my deepest

reservoir of truth;
It is my well of living water.

Paula D'Arcy

Our home in Watertown

On honeymoon, 1973

Sarah, just before the accident

Paula with Beth Starr